W9-ALJ-228

Pebble™ Plus

Healthy Eating with MyPyramid

The Vegetable Group

by Mari C. Schuh

Consulting Editor: Gail Saunders-Smith, PhD

Consultant: Barbara J. Rolls, PhD
Guthrie Chair in Nutrition
The Pennsylvania State University
University Park, Pennsylvania

Capstone press
Mankato, Minnesota

Pebble Plus is published by Capstone Press,
151 Good Counsel Drive, P.O. Box 669, Mankato, Minnesota 56002.
www.capstonepress.com

1 2 3 4 5 6 11 10 09 08 07 06

Library of Congress Cataloging-in-Publication Data
Schuh, Mari C., 1975–
    The vegetable group / by Mari C. Schuh.
    p. cm.—(Pebble plus. Healthy eating with MyPyramid)
    Summary: "Simple text and photographs present the vegetable group, the foods in this group,
and examples of healthy eating choices"—Provided by publisher.
    Includes bibliographical references and index.
    ISBN-13: 978-0-7368-5374-3 (hardcover)
    ISBN-10: 0-7368-5374-X (hardcover)
    1. Vegetables—Juvenile literature. 2. Nutrition—Juvenile literature. I. Title. II. Series.
TX557.S38 2006
641.3'5—dc22   2005023427

Credits
Jennifer Bergstrom, designer; Kelly Garvin, photo researcher; Stacy Foster and Michelle Biedscheid,
        photo shoot coordinators

Photo Credits
BananaStock Ltd., 1; Capstone Press/Karon Dubke, cover, 3, 5, 9, 11, 13, 15, 16–17, 18–19, 21, 22 (all);
Corbis/Andreas von Einsiedel/Elizabeth Whiting & Associates, 15 (background), 19 (background); Corbis/
Ariel Skelley, 6–7; Getty Images Inc./Patti McConville, 5 (background), 21 (background); U.S. Department
of Agriculture, 8, 9 (inset)

The author dedicates this book to Mapleton librarian Bonnie Klein and her husband, Karl, whose vegetable
garden is larger than the library where she works.

**Information in this book supports the U.S. Department of Agriculture's MyPyramid for Kids
food guidance system found at http://www.MyPyramid.gov/kids. Food amounts listed in this
book are based on an 1,800-calorie food plan.**

**The U.S. Department of Agriculture (USDA) does not endorse any products, services,
or organizations.**

Note to Parents and Teachers

The Healthy Eating with MyPyramid set supports national science standards related to
nutrition and physical health. This book describes and illustrates the vegetable group.
The images support early readers in understanding the text. The repetition of words and
phrases helps early readers learn new words. This book also introduces early readers
to subject-specific vocabulary words, which are defined in the Glossary section. Early
readers may need assistance to read some words and to use the Table of Contents,
Glossary, Read More, Internet Sites, and Index sections of the book.

Table of Contents

Vegetables

How many vegetables
have you eaten today?

Did you know that vegetables
come from plants?
Vegetables help keep you
healthy and strong.

MyPyramid for Kids

MyPyramid teaches you
how much to eat
from each food group.
Vegetables are one
food group in MyPyramid.

MyPyramid For Kids
Eat Right. Exercise. Have Fun.

To learn more about
healthy eating, go
to this web site:
www.MyPyramid.gov/kids
Ask an adult for help.

Kids should eat
at least 2½ cups
of vegetables every day.

Enjoying Vegetables

Cucumbers, carrots, cabbage.

There are all kinds

of vegetables.

If you don't like one,

try another.

Yellow, red, green.

See how many colors

you can eat.

Corn, tomatoes, and lettuce

are part of a healthy meal.

Crunch, crunch, crunch.

Carrots and celery

make a fun snack.

You can make

a vegetable pizza.

Top it with peppers

and mushrooms.

Vegetables are part
of a healthy meal.
What are your
favorite vegetables?

How Much to Eat

Kids need to eat at least 2½ cups of vegetables every day. To get 2½ cups, pick five of your favorite vegetables below.

Pick five of your favorite vegetables to eat today!

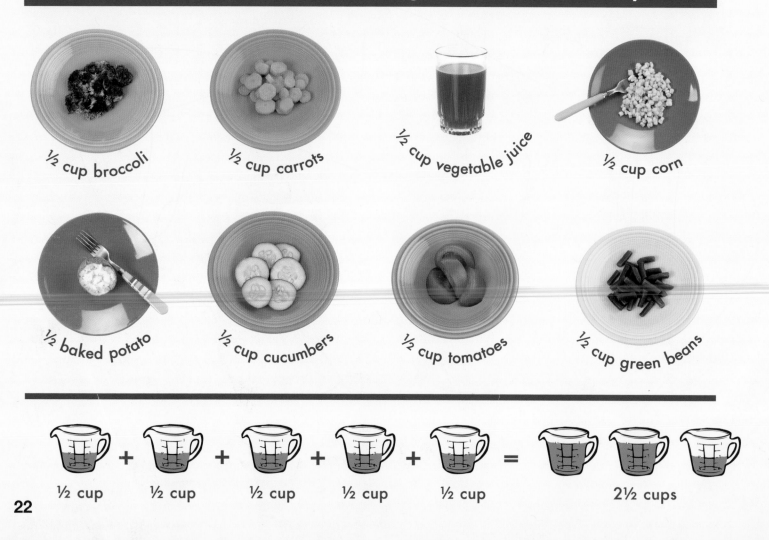

½ cup broccoli

½ cup carrots

½ cup vegetable juice

½ cup corn

½ baked potato

½ cup cucumbers

½ cup tomatoes

½ cup green beans

½ cup + ½ cup + ½ cup + ½ cup + ½ cup = 2½ cups

Glossary

MyPyramid—a food plan that helps kids make healthy food choices and reminds kids to be active; MyPyramid was created by the U.S. Department of Agriculture.

snack—a small amount of food people eat when they are hungry between meals

vegetable—a part of a plant that people eat; vegetables come from many parts of a plant; vegetables can be roots, stems, leaves, flowers, or seeds.

Read More

Klingel, Cynthia, and Robert B. Noyed. *Vegetables.* Let's Read About Food. Milwaukee: Weekly Reader Early Learning Library, 2002.

Rondeau, Amanda. *Vegetables Are Vital.* What Should I Eat? Edina, Minn.: Abdo, 2003.

Thomas, Ann. *Vegetables.* Food. Philadelphia: Chelsea Clubhouse, 2003.

Index

Internet Sites

FactHound offers a safe, fun way to find Internet sites related to this book. All of the sites on FactHound have been researched by our staff.

Here's how:

1. Visit *www.facthound.com*

2. Type in this special code **073685374X** for age-appropriate sites. Or enter a search word related to this book for a more general search.

3. Click on the **Fetch It** button.

FactHound will fetch the best sites for you!

Word Count: 121
Grade: 1
Early-Intervention Level: 13